ID
of Yesteryear

Mavis Piller

OBELISK PUBLICATIONS

OTHER TITLES IN THIS SERIES

Ashburton of Yesteryear, *John Germon and Pete Webb*
The Teign Valley of Yesteryear, Parts I and II, *Chips Barber*
Brixham of Yesteryear, Parts I, II and III, *Chips Barber*
Pinhoe of Yesteryear, Parts I and II, *Chips Barber*
Princetown of Yesteryear, Parts I and II, *Chips Barber*
Kingsteignton of Yesteryear, *Richard Harris*
Heavitree of Yesteryear, *Chips Barber*
Kenton and Starcross of Yesteryear, *Eric Vaughan*
Exmouth Century, Parts One and Two, *George Pridmore*

OTHER TITLES ABOUT THIS AREA

Around & About the Haldon Hills – Revisited, *Chips Barber*
The Lost City of Exeter – Revisited, *Chips Barber*
The Great Little Exeter Book, *Chips Barber*
Beautiful Exeter, *Chips Barber*
An Exeter Boyhood, *Frank Retter*
The Ghosts of Exeter, *Sally and Chips Barber*
Topsham Past and Present, *Chips Barber*
Ian Jubb's Exeter Collection
An Alphington Album, *Pauline Aplin and Jeanne Gaskell*
Exploring Exeter – The Heart of the City, *Jean Maun*
Exploring Exeter – The West Quarter, *Jean Maun*
Around the Churches of Exeter, *Walter Jacobson*

We have over 160 Devon titles; for a full list please send an SAE to
Obelisk Publications, 2 Church Hill, Pinhoe, Exeter EX4 9ER

Acknowledgements

Thanks to Edna Conbeer for helping to date some of the pictures. Thanks also to John Sculpher for picture on page 31 (bottom) and to Chips Barber for pictures on page 4.

First published in 2000 by
Obelisk Publications, 2 Church Hill, Pinhoe, Exeter, Devon
Designed and Typeset by Sally Barber
Printed in Great Britain

IDE *of Yesteryear*

Ide may only be a small village with a population of well under a thousand, but it is a village full of character! Over a period of years (more than I care to remember) I have collected picture postcards of this lovely place and, in this book, have put together a pictorial record of some of the finest, often unrepeatable, images of Ide ever published. I hope you will share the same joy in looking at them that I have had in collecting them.

This book is a photographic journey rather than a history text and follows a rough sequence from just outside the village boundary on the edge of Exeter, through its heart and beyond. There are also a number of pictures featuring villagers, many of them taken when they were children at the village school. If you are a true 'local' then there will certainly be some faces that you will recognise. I hope they revive some pleasant memories for you.

Many of the scenes are from picture postcards which I have bought at postcard fairs or collected from other sources. Some are 'new', i.e. never sent, presumably bought originally as a keepsake when few people owned a camera. Others have been through the postal system and wherever possible I have given the dates when they have been sent. Although this does not give an exact year when the picture was taken, it does give an indication of the age of the scene. In the days when phones were rare (leave alone faxes and e-mails) it was quite common to send a card first thing in the morning, which was delivered the same day!

Before we start our journey, here is an instant reminder of a bygone age as 'one horse-power' of environmentally friendly transport makes its way along the 'watersplash'.

REMEMBER THAT
FOR MANY HUNDRED YEARS
THIS WAS
A BEAUTIFUL VALLEY
WHERE PEOPLE COULD
MAKE THEIR WAY TO IDE
THROUGH GREEN FIELDS
AND BY THE SIDE
OF A RUNNING BROOK

IT WAS DESTROYED IN 1974
BY THE DEPARTMENT
OF THE ENVIRONMENT
GEOFFREY RIPPON M.P.
JOHN PEYTON M.P.
KIETH SPEED M.P.
BRIGADIER BALDWIN

RESOLVE THAT YOUR
GENERATION SHALL LEAVE
ENGLAND A MORE
BEAUTIFUL PLACE THAN
THEY FOUND IT AND UNDO
THE VANDALISM OF OURS

One of the biggest intrusions into Ide life occurred in 1974 when the A30 dual carriageway was built along the valley of the Alphin Brook. The top two pictures show the Bridge Inn (now the Twisted Oak), and the 'tombstone' or memorial erected near it to commemorate the spoiling of the valley by this road, whilst below is the scene as it is now with the road 'carving' its way through the landscape. On the opposite page the top picture shows Holmbush Cottage, whilst the bottom two are similar, but not identical, views of the bridge.

IDE.

Ide of Yesteryear

(Opposite top) This shows Ide's War Memorial many decades before the spiralling footbridge was built over the 1974 road. The middle and bottom pictures are two similar views along Fore Street, with quite a few years in between. On this page there are more views of Fore Street. The top picture was posted in August 1908 to Fareham in Hampshire by the person staying in the house marked by an 'x'. Next door is the shop owned by Cox, also featured in the middle picture. Apparently Cox's bakery business served quite a wide area beyond the village limits and orders were taken as far afield as Tedburn St Mary and to remote houses in the Haldon area. The bottom picture shows what the roads were like when they were unsurfaced.

The common theme of the pictures across these two pages is the Huntsman Inn. Emily Wren, who kept the pub for more than forty years, is shown pulling a pint in 1968 and is also, albeit somewhat younger, in the picture beside it. The pictures also reveal the amazing length of the inn's sign, which spans the width of the building.

(Above) The pub's owners 'Well Park Brewery' have advertised their ales and stout. This brewery was in Willey's Avenue but it later became a bathroom centre.

(Below) The Huntsman lives up to its name in this picture from the 1950s.

Here are two old views of Ide's famous ford or 'watersplash'. The bottom picture was posted on 3 July 1905 to Balham in London and the sender recorded that the weather in Ide was glorious. The top view with its small herd of cows was, perhaps appropriately, sent to a Mr Butcher in Bournemouth.

Where Fore Street ends, the High Street begins. The top view is from an age when there was no motor traffic to threaten the quiet of the village's main street. A group of youngsters have had their curiosity aroused by the rare presence of a photographer and seem keen to get in on the action. The young man on the left is not holding a loaf of bread on a tray, but is pushing a baby in a pram!

The bottom view, looking back down the High Street from just above the Old Mill (long ago a corn mill but for many years a restaurant), is much more recent and is the work of the late Arthur Luxton, who took several picture postcard views of the village.

On this pair of pages it's possible to see a row of cottages on the left of the picture above, which is looking up the High Street and, on the right side of the picture below, looking down the street. They no longer exist as disaster befell them in late July 1930. The *Western Times* reported the fire which destroyed them: '*Early Wednesday afternoon fire broke out in one of a block of four very old thatched cottages at Ide near the school. In a short time the flames spread to the adjoining three cottages and continued to burn fiercely during the afternoon ...*

Exeter Fire Brigade quickly got to work. Plenty of water was obtained from a mill pond but a stiff breeze fanned the flames, and it was soon apparent that it was impossible to save the remaining cottages from total destruction.

Villagers, however, turned out as soon as the alarm was raised and rendered valuable help, and succeeded in removing a considerable quantity of furniture in the three cottages to which the the fire extended.

Great anxiety was felt for the school, which was only a few yards off. The children had

only just entered the school for the afternoon session. As a precautionary measure they were removed to a part of the building farthest from the burning cottages.

The Fire Brigade played on another thatched cottage hard by, belonging to Mrs Swabey, which appeared to be in danger, but fortunately the wind blew the flames in a contrary direction.

The four cottages destroyed are known as Lock's Cottages. The owner is Mrs Pope, a widow, who with three children, occupied number 2; and Nos 1, 3, and 4 were tenanted respectively by Mrs Hall, a widow; Mr Sims, a naval pensioner, who, it's understood, had one child stopping with him; and Mr Johns, with whom were his wife and two young children. All are homeless, but are being accommodated temporarily by neighbours.

Ide Parochial Committee resolved itself into an emergency meeting of the Parish Council, to consider what action should be taken to help the families rendered homeless … The conflagration is the largest that has befallen the village since 1710, when fourteen cottages were destroyed …'

Here we are still in the almost deserted High Street, these two views looking in opposite directions. The top one shows yet another of the village's former shops, Glanville Stores. There are three people on the right-hand side of the bottom picture. In the window of the property beside them is a single word on a printed card saying 'Tea'.

It's hardly surprising that there is nobody in the top view (opposite) with snow on the road and rooftops – it's obviously a cold and wintry scene. The house behind the lamp

standard is Verandah Cottage, where my grandmother lived, and myself in later years, and holds many personal memories. Courtney's shop on the left has now gone. The message on the card was addressed 'The Stores, Ide' and was sent on 31 December 1920 to Nurse E. Wren who worked at the 'Mental Hospital, Wells, Somerset'. The message simply said, 'With every good wish for the New Year. From L. Courtney.' The card sent to my mother so long ago is now with me.

Below we are still at the top of the High Street and the New Inn (now the Poachers) can be spied on the right.

The picture in the centre-page spread is of The Green, a peaceful retreat behind the High Street and close to St Ida's Church.

The top view appeared on a postcard sent on 9 April 1907 and the opening line was 'What do you think of this view?' We'll never know the reply but the road is little more than a dirt track, so the suggestion may have been that this was being noted as a rural backwater. Below is another cottage no longer in existence. Chilleys Farm stood beside the road at West Town but was destroyed by enemy action during the Second World War. Opposite is a composite card showing four Ide scenes: the bridge, the inside and outside of St Ida's Church and the village school. The card, published by Currie and Cliffe, of Teignmouth, was posted on Christmas Eve 1906, from Alphington!

The Coronation of George VI, in 1937, was celebrated in some style at Ide when many folk donned their finest clothes to enjoy a tea-party. Below, the village's football team, Ide AFC of 1924, is seen posed here with several trophies, two on the ground and another held by the sport-loving, cricket-crazy Rev. Harold Wake Millett, who had become Vicar of Ide in 1919.

Left is a former headmaster of the village school, either Mr Jewell or Mr William Ashton, shown here in about 1924, teaching a lesson about the geography of the North Sea.

Above it's those not-so-lazy-hazy days of June 1966 when Ide Sports Day saw these youngsters in action.

Below is the first of a number of pictures of pupils, from a wide span of years, who attended school in Ide.

The picture above is from about 1918 and shows the children staying as still as they could whilst the photographer tried his best to capture them for posterity.

Below we have moved on some eight years as this picture was dated 1926, and the expressions look decidedly more cheerful.

Ide of Yesteryear

According to the note on the back of the above photo this picture, published by the Scholastic Souvenir Company of Blackpool, features 'Class 3', whose teacher was Mrs Henson.

Below, the picture, taken just before Christmas 1956, is of 'Class 4', taught by Mrs Albon.

Ide's school has, for a primary school, quite a large catchment area and many of the pupils featured here lived well outside the village, coming from such places as Whitestone, Holcombe Burnell and Longdown. Here are two more pictures from the 1950s and most have managed a smiling face for the photographer. Mrs Wykes is the teacher in both pictures.

Our last two school pictures again feature a number of familiar faces and the pupils seem to be getting bigger. In the bottom picture, which is from Christmas 1967, the pupils are mostly in school uniform apart, notably, from the young man, at the centre of the action, who is holding a handbell, apparently ready to make an important announcement.

More than half a century has elapsed since these would-be actors and actresses 'trod the boards'. The caption on the back of the bottom one of these late 1940s pictures says that the 'show' was performed both at Ide and at the Buller Hall in nearby Exeter. Here the show's cast are taking a well-deserved bow at the end of their performance.

The picture above is a reminder that in past times the villagers of Ide derived their livelihood from the land. In those days of yesteryear horses, either as transport or as working animals, were a common sight in and around the village.

Below is the large farmhouse of Canns Farm, a Grade II listed building dating back to 1859 and located at the top of the village. This farm was, at the beginning of the nineteenth century, the fourth largest in the village with 113 acres. Since this photograph was taken, many years ago, improvements have been made to the property. Time marches on!

The picture above predates the one below. The differences are numerous so you may like to spot the changes for yourself. The late Professor Hoskins, in his mammoth book *Devon*, published in 1954, said of it: *'The church, entirely rebuilt in 1834, is poor inside and out. The Vicarage … is more attractive.'*

This you can judge for yourself on seeing these old picture postcard views. The top one was posted on 31 October 1912 by someone staying in the village at Rosemont Cottage and gave us the information that 'the village has about 680 people'. Some of them can be seen in the bottom picture!

The 'Teign Valley Railway', as most people seem to refer to it, ran from Exeter through Alphington, climbing past the top of Ide and beyond along a valley to Perridge, below Longdown, through two tunnels, one long, one short, and into the Teign Valley. Having passed many country stations, the line ran into the small railway junction at Heathfield. When the coastal main-line route was closed it offered an alternative way, for west-bound passengers, of travelling by rail between Exeter and Newton Abbot. There are many pictures of this line featured in two other books in this series, *The Teign Valley of Yesteryear* (parts I and II). The top picture postcard view was sent on 22 August 1905, not long after the line opened. The railway, for economic reasons, ceased running in 1958 and its passing was lamented by many.

In its short working life the history of this branch line, described by some as a 'tin-pot railway', proved to be a colourful one, and a favourite for those who liked a sedate ride through lovely countryside. The picture here dates back to 2 July 1938 and shows a group of holiday-makers who had elected to stay in the camping coach shown on the left side of the picture. The first camping coaches on this line appeared in 1934 and there were others at Ashton and Chudleigh. With these 'happy campers' is Bert Beer.

Below is the 'Ide Express', an elaborate entry for St Thomas Carnival many years ago. There is some debate as to how far this vehicle, possibly adapted from the first tractor to be used in the village, actually got, as reports seem to conflict. One body of opinion has it only reaching the Falmouth Inn, near the crossroads at the bottom of Dunsford Hill. However, a report written a few days after the event stated that: *'One of the most interesting tableaux at the St Thomas Carnival was "The London-Ide Express," which secured the first prize for the most original turn-out. This tableau was arranged by Messrs F. C. Gilpin, W. H. Braddon, A. Wilkes and J. Ryan ... the "passengers" included J. Jewell, A. Farley, F. Wren, D. Nuth, E. Jewell, W. A. Jewell and S. Blake. The tractor was kindly lent by Mr J. Benyon.'*

The view above, posted 21 July 1909, shows the railway line passing along the top of the village. Ide's small station can be seen, on a bend, in the distance. The picture below takes us almost back to where we started this photographic journey. Here we stand looking across the valley towards Ide. Pole House is on the left and there is no dual carriageway in this lovely rural scene of rolling hills.

I do hope you enjoyed looking at these pictures of 'Ide of Yesteryear'. Why not take the book on a walk around the village and compare the pictures with how it is now? You might find a few surprises along the way!

Ide of Yesteryear